MW01008832

NUMBER THE STARS

by
Lois Lowry

Teacher Guide

Written by
Phyllis A. Green

Note

The Dell Yearling paperback edition of the book was used to prepare this guide. The page references may differ in the hardcover or other paperback editions.

Please note: Please assess the appropriateness of this book for the age level and maturity of your students prior to reading and discussing it with your class.

ISBN 978-1-56137-254-6

To order, contact your local school supply store, or—
Novel Units, Inc.
P.O. Box 97
Bulverde, TX 78163-0097

Web site: www.novelunits.com

Table of Contents

Skills and Strategies

Thinking
Comparing/contrasting,
evaluating, analyzing details,
synthesizing ideas

Literary Elements
Character, setting, plot
development, story map,
figurative language, symbol,
point of view, personification

Vocabulary
Sorting, context clues,
metacognition, categorizing

Comprehension
Predicting, sequencing,
cause/effect, inference,
compare information from
more than one source

Writing
Narrative, expository

Listening/Speaking
Participation in discussion
and cooperative groups,
participation in
dramatization and role play

Summary of *Number the Stars*

Number the Stars is set in Denmark in 1943 during the Nazi occupation. Annemarie Johansen and Ellen Rosen are ten-year-old best friends. Their lives are affected by the circumstances of the times—food shortages, anti-Semitism, and soldiers patrolling their neighborhood. The Johansen family assists the Rosens in their flight to Sweden with Annemarie going on a dangerous errand. *Number the Stars* is the 1990 Newbery Award Medal Winner.

About the Newbery Award

The medal is named for eighteenth-century British bookseller John Newbery. It is awarded annually by the Association for Library Service to Children, a division of the American Library Association, to the author of the most distinguished contribution to American literature for children.

About the Author

Lois Lowry has penned many favorite titles for young people. She is author of the well-loved Anastasia series as well as *All About Sam*.

Initiating Activities

Several suggestions are included; the teacher may choose for his/her particular students.
1. Provide nonfiction background on the Second World War occupation of Denmark, the Resistance, and the Holocaust. Elicit student predictions about the book. Divide students into pairs to prepare three questions about the book.

2. Hold up a Star of David. Explain that it is significant in the story. Then ask students to predict why. Save the predictions on chart paper to use after reading the book.

3. This book is a Newbery Winner. What do you expect of it?

4. Look at the cover and end notes. What are your predictions about the book?

5. Read the first few pages of the book aloud and then allow students to read silently. When they've completed the first chapter, record first impressions and make some predictions.

Using Predictions

We all make predictions as we read—little guesses about what will happen next, how a conflict will be resolved, which details will be important to the plot, which details will help fill in our sense of a character. Students should be encouraged to predict, to make sensible guesses as they read the novel.

As students work on their predictions, these discussion questions can be used to guide them: What are some of the ways to predict? What is the process of a sophisticated reader's thinking and predicting? What clues does an author give to help us make predictions? Why are some predictions more likely to be accurate than others?

Create a chart for recording predictions. This could be either an individual or class activity. As each subsequent chapter is discussed, students can review and correct their previous predictions about plot and characters as necessary.

Use the facts and ideas the author gives.

Use your own prior knowledge.

Apply any new information (i.e., from class discussion) that may cause you to change your mind.

Predictions

_____

_____

_____

_____

Prediction Chart

What characters have we met so far?	What is the conflict in the story?	What are your predictions?	Why did you make those predictions?

Teacher Background Information

World War II (1939-1945)
It destroyed more property, killed more people (military deaths totalled 17 million with even greater civilian deaths), and disrupted more lives than any other war in history. The war began on September 1, 1939, when Germany invaded Poland. Germany's dictator, Adolf Hitler, had built Germany into a powerful war machine which crushed Poland, Denmark, Luxembourg, the Netherlands, Belgium, Norway, and France. Germany, Italy, and Japan formed an alliance known as the Axis. Germany surrendered on May 7, 1945, and Japan on September 2, 1945.

Tivoli Gardens
Copenhagen is famous for its Tivoli Gardens amusement park. The park opened in 1843 and offers ballet and pantomime, rides and shooting galleries, restaurants, circus acts, concerts, and fireworks displays.

Nazism
Political movement developed in Germany during the 1920s. It later became a form of government with dictator Adolf Hitler from 1933 to 1945.

Star of David
The Star of David is the universal symbol of Judaism. It appears on the Israeli flag, in synagogues, and on Jewish objects.

Rosh Hashanah
It is the Jewish New Year celebration which usually begins in September, on the first day of the Hewbrew month of Tishri. During the two day celebration, Jews pray for God's forgiveness, for a good year, and for long life. Rosh Hashanah begins the Ten Days of Penitence which end on Yom Kippur, the Day of Atonement. Jews attend synagogue services on Rosh Hashanah.

Denmark in World War II
On April 9, 1940, German forces invaded Denmark and the Danes surrendered after a few hours of fighting. Initially the Germans allowed the Danish government to continue, but took over the government in August 1943. In September 1943, the Danes organized the secret Freedom Council to lead the resistance movement which had developed since 1940. The Freedom Council helped about 7,000 Danish Jews escape to Sweden.

Story Map

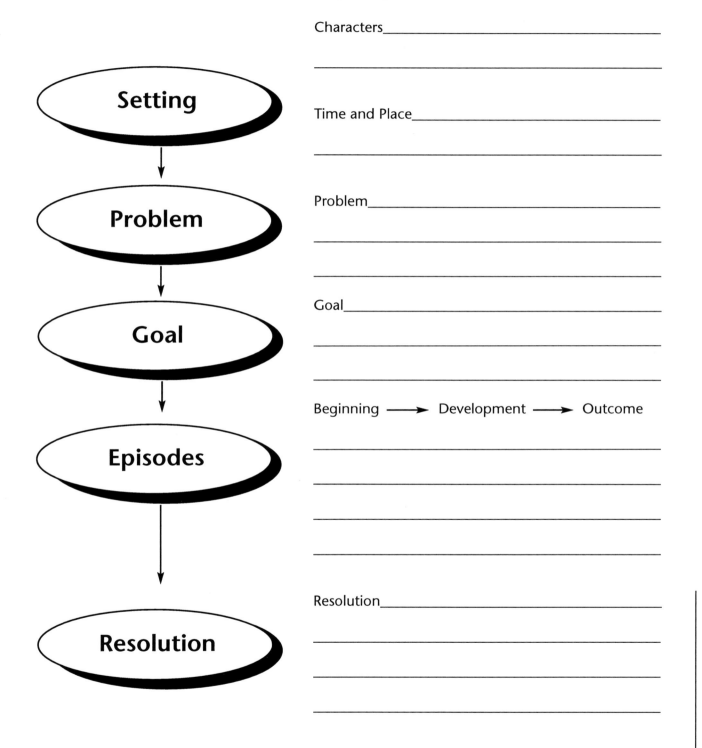

Characters_____

_____

Time and Place_____

_____

Problem_____

_____

_____

Goal_____

_____

_____

Beginning ⟶ Development ⟶ Outcome

_____

_____

_____

_____

Resolution_____

_____

_____

_____

Chapter-by-Chapter
Vocabulary, Discussion Questions, and Activities

Chapter 1   "Why Are You Running?"—Pages 1-10

Vocabulary

lanky 1	rucksack 1	plodding 2	contempt 3
sneering 3	obstinate 4	hoodlums 5	sabotage 8
impassive 10			

Discussion Questions

1. How are Annemarie and Ellen similar to ten-year-olds you know today? How are their lives different?

Similar	Different
• running to prepare for school races • carry school books • leave younger sibling behind • make up names for other people (Giraffe)	• they see soldiers daily who can stop and question them • food shortages—butter, coffee, sugar

2. Who were the Resistance fighters? *(Danish people who brought harm to the Nazis in sneaky guerrilla-type ways.)*

3. Why does Mrs. Rosen tell the girls to walk another way to school? *(to avoid the German soldiers)*

4. How does Lowry convey the attitudes of the girls and their mothers toward the German soldiers and vice versa? Cite examples from Chapter 1.

   Directly: • "ordered in a stern voice" (page 2)

   In Words: • "Annemarie thought with contempt" (page 3)
                          • "sneering" (page 3)
                          • "her mother asked anxiously" (page 6)
                          • "uneasy looks" (page 7)

   By Actions: • "the shopkeeper move...out of sight." (page 3)

   By Conversation: • The girls decide not to tell their mothers about the soldiers. (page 6)
                          • "They will remember your faces. It is important to be one of the crowd, always." (page 8)

   By Way of Talking: • "She spoke in a low voice to Ellen's mother." (page 7)

Supplementary Activities

1. Notice how Lois Lowry starts the book. Why do you think she used dialogue as her beginning? Answer in a sentence or two. What are some other ways to start books?

2. **Visualization:** Draw a picture of the Copenhagen neighborhood of the story. There is a word description on page 7 to help you.

Chapter 2   "Who Is the Man Who Rides Past?"—Pages 11-17

Vocabulary
trousseau 14   intricate 14

Discussion Questions

1. Who is King Christian X? *(The King of Denmark)* Why doesn't he need a designated bodyguard? *(because all of Denmark protects him)*

2. Why does King Christian X ride around Copenhagen on his horse? *(to cheer his citizens and as a symbol to the occupying German soldiers of the King of Denmark)* Why are symbols important? *(Answers vary.)*

3. Who is Hans Christian Andersen? *(A Danish author of fairy tales who lived from 1805-1875.)*

4. Look in the chapter for a comparison between the fairy tale king and King Christian X's actions. Why does an author use such a device? *(Answers vary, but include the notion that such comparisons make the author's ideas and plot more vivid. Inconsistencies seem stronger.)*

5. There is a bit of extra white space on page 16. Why? *(to make the break of three years and to make the contrast more pointed)*

6. How had things changed in the three years? *(King Christian X was older and had been injured when he fell from his horse. Lise had died in an accident two weeks before her wedding. Peter was more somber.)*

Supplementary Activities

1. Lowry says, "The whole world had changed. Only the fairy tales remained the same." Discuss what the author means. Use example of your own or ones you've heard about. Newscasts or newspapers may offer possible examples.

2. King Christian X is a symbol of a free Denmark. What are some other symbols you know about? Generate a class list.

Chapter 3   "Where Is Mrs. Hirsch?"—Pages 18-26

Vocabulary

rationed 18   haughtily 19   sarcastically 21   swastika 21   curfew 22

Discussion Questions

1. How do shortages affect Annemarie and Ellen? *(Lack of fuel meant they had to heat their building using an old chimney. Electricity was rationed so they used candles.)*

2. What is rationing? *(Limiting various commodities such as fuel, food or sugar to a certain amount per person or family.)*

3. Why are there shortages in the story? *(During the war, the usual commerce, business, and manufacturing is stopped. Efforts go toward the war only.)*

4. Where is Mrs. Hirsch? *(The author doesn't tell us where she has gone, only that her button and thread shop has been closed by the Germans.)*

5. Why is Kirsti's explanation of where the Hirsches have gone different from Ellen and Annemarie's understanding? *(She is younger, more naive, and less aware of the real situation in Copenhagen.)*

6. What is the mood of Peter's visit? *(secret, against the curfew so dangerous, serious)*

7. What revelation comes to Annemarie at the end of Chapter 3? *(The Rosens are Jewish and may be in danger.)*

8. Who will guard Denmark's Jews? *(all of Denmark as in the bodyguard for King Christian X)*

9. Reread the last paragraph of Chapter 3. What are Annemarie's feelings? *(concerned, but removed from the action herself)* What do you predict in the rest of the story?

Chapter 4   "It Will Be a Long Night"—Pages 27-38

Vocabulary

sophisticated 27	exasperated 28	belligerently 31	ablaze 31
submerged 32	tense 33	dismay 34	dubiously 34
tension 35			

Discussion Questions

1. In Chapter 4, the three girls sometimes play and act as children and sometimes are serious and act as adults. Make a list of activities in each category.

Childlike Play	Adultlike
• played paper dolls • acted out *Gone With the Wind* characters • Kirsti believes the explosions were for her birthday	• Ellen suggested a way to improve Kirsti's fish skin shoes • be told of the danger to the Danish Jews and the Rosens • figure out what to say if questioned

2. What happened to the Tivoli Gardens? *(The German occupation forces had burned part of it.)*

3. Why were there explosions on Kirsti's fifth birthday? *(The Danish King had blown up his navel fleet so the Germans couldn't take over the ships.)*

4. Why do the Johansens have a large chicken dinner in Chapter 4 and Mr. Johansen has three daughters again? *(The Rosens have fled and Ellen is staying with the Johansen's.)*

5. How could Peter help the Rosens? *(Answers vary.)* Look for clues in the book about Peter. *(He comes quickly and talks secretly. He gives beer, sea shells, and underground newspapers to the Johansens. He comes in spite of the curfew.)*

Supplementary Activity

Start attribute webs for the characters in the book. (See pages 12-16.)

Using Character Webs

Attribute webs are simply a visual representation of a character from the novel. They provide a systematic way for students to organize and recap the information they have about a particular character. Attribute webs may be used after reading the novel to recapitulate information about a particular character, or completed gradually as information unfolds. They may be completed individually or as a group project.

One type of character attribute web uses these divisions:

- How a character acts and feels. (How does the character act? How do you think the character feels? How would you feel if this happened to you?)

- How a character looks. (Close your eyes and picture the character. Describe him/her to me.)

- Where a character lives. (Where and when does the character live?)

- How others feel about the character. (How does another specific character feel about our character?)

In group discussion about the characters described in student attribute webs, the teacher can ask for backup proof from the novel. Inferential thinking can be included in the discussion.

Attribute webs need not be confined to characters. They may also be used to organize information about a concept, object, or place.

Attribute Web

The attribute web below will help you gather clues the author provides about a character in the novel. Fill in the blanks with words and phrases which tell how the character acts and looks, as well as what the character says and what others say about him or her.

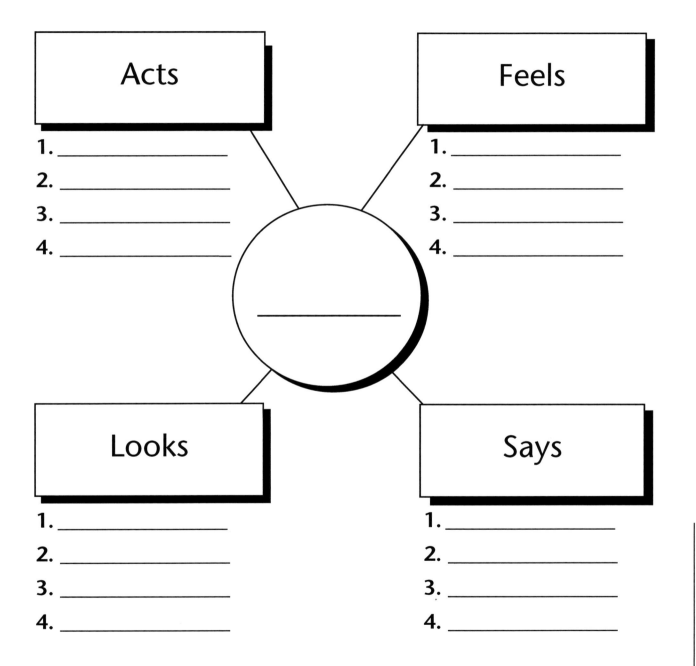

Acts

1. _____
2. _____
3. _____
4. _____

Feels

1. _____
2. _____
3. _____
4. _____

Looks

1. _____
2. _____
3. _____
4. _____

Says

1. _____
2. _____
3. _____
4. _____

Attribute Web

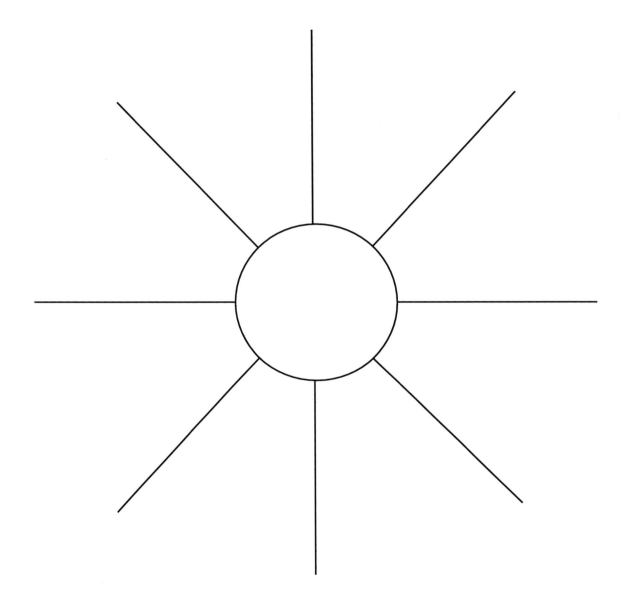

Completed Attribute Webs

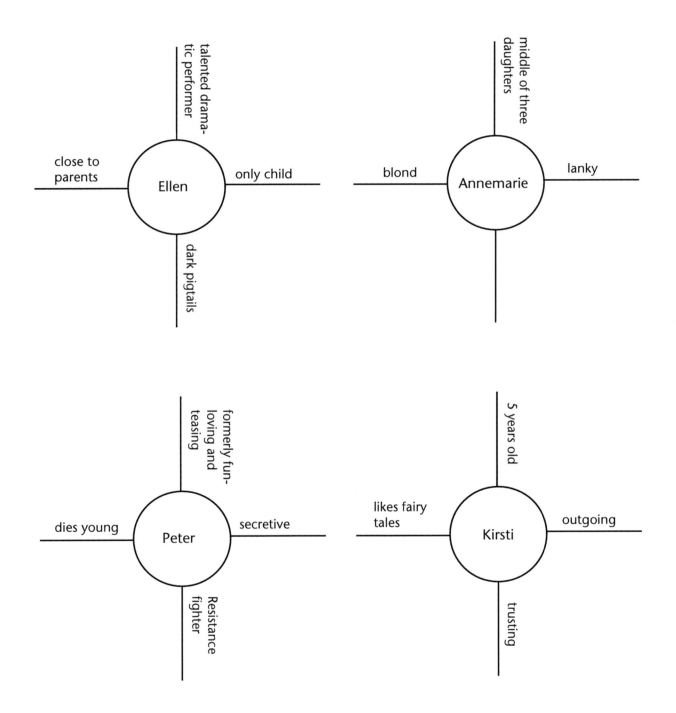

Ellen
- talented dramatic performer
- only child
- dark pigtails
- close to parents

Annemarie
- middle of three daughters
- lanky
- blond

Peter
- formerly fun-loving and teasing
- secretive
- Resistance fighter
- dies young

Kirsti
- 5 years old
- outgoing
- trusting
- likes fairy tales

Completed Attribute Webs

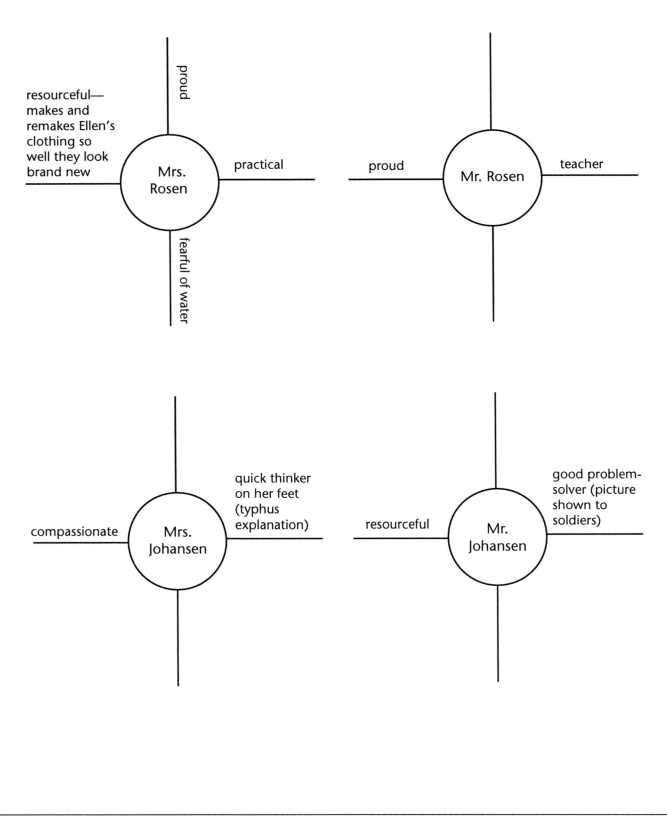

resourceful—makes and remakes Ellen's clothing so well they look brand new

proud

Mrs. Rosen

practical

fearful of water

proud

Mr. Rosen

teacher

compassionate

Mrs. Johansen

quick thinker on her feet (typhus explanation)

resourceful

Mr. Johansen

good problem-solver (picture shown to soldiers)

Chapter 5   "Who Is the Dark-Haired One?"—Pages 39-49

Vocabulary
imperious 39   intoned 39   stalk 44

Discussion Questions
1. Why did the night in Chapter 5 seem different from a normal night? *(Ellen Rosen was staying with the Johansens and all were fearful of the German soldiers.)*

2. *Why does Annemarie feel "completely safe" when she goes to sleep? (She is in her own bed and her own home with her parents in the next room and her best friend beside her.)* How do you think Ellen feels? *(Answers vary.)*

3. What is Papa's manner to the soldiers in the middle of the night? *(brusk, matter-of fact, disrespectful)*

4. What is the significance of the Star of David in this chapter? *(The symbol of Judaism is on a gold chain around Ellen's neck and would betray the truth to the soldiers if it were seen.)*

5. Reread the last paragraphs in Chapters 3 and 5. How has the situation for Annemarie changed? What do you predict for the rest of the book?

Supplementary Activities
1. Dramatize the chapter.

2. The Star of David is a symbol of Judaism. What is a symbol? Make a list of other symbols. Choose one to explain in a short paragraph. *(eagle, cross, shamrock, wings, owl)*

Chapter 6   "Is the Weather Good for Fishing?"—Pages 50-59

Vocabulary
tentatively 50   mourning 56   sprawling 56   massive 56
exasperation 57   pranced 57

Discussion Questions
1. What was puzzling about Papa's telephone conversation with Henrik? *(They talked of cigarettes being available in Copenhagen even though Annemarie was quite sure there were no cigarettes available.)*

2. On page 55, "Annemarie tensed." Why does Annemarie feel apprehensive? Why is Annemarie concerned about Kirsti? *(Kirsti is only five and too young to understand about being guarded around the German soldiers.)*

3. Look at a map to identify the places mentioned in the story. Be sure to recognize the distances between locations.

4. Describe the area the group walks through after leaving the train. (pages 56-59) What feeling does the author give about that area? *(calm, pleasant, safe)* How does Lowry convey the feeling?

Directly:
- "lovely and fresh"
- "pretty"

Association:
- Mother reminisced about the area and past pleasant experiences.

Detail:
- "low stone wall"
- "few flowering bushes"
- "chrysanthemums"

Supplementary Activity
Personification is giving human characteristics to inanimate objects or nonhumans. Find examples in the book. *(Page 56, "High against the pale clouds, seagulls soared and cried out as if they were mourning.")*

Chapter 7   "The House by the Sea"—Pages 60-66

Vocabulary
awe 60   gnarled 60   appliqued 65

Discussion Questions
1. What is Annemarie's mood at the start of Chapter 7? *(carefree, happy)* How does she convey her mood to Ellen? *(Verbally she says how beautiful her uncle's house and the land on the sea is. With actions she shows Ellen the area, running in the meadow and testing the water with their toes. Conversationally the two girls chatter about the sea and the city and picture two girls in Sweden looking across to Denmark.)*

2. How is Mama's manner in contrast to Annemarie's? *(Mama is concerned that no one see the girls and inquire about Ellen. German soldiers are also a concern.)*

3. Why does Annemarie comment on page 64 that it is not a bad time? *(The girls will be well fed with applesauce and fish.)*

4. What is Ellen's mood in Chapter 7? *(She is lonely for her parents. She misses her Star of David which Annemarie has hidden.)*

5. Why was there a difference in the mood between Mama and Henrik in Chapter 7? *(There was no laughter. The times were serious and dangerous.)*

6. What do you predict for the rest of the book? Why did Mama take the girls to visit her brother?

Supplementary Activities
1. Art: Draw a picture of the house by the sea.

2. Investigate Scandinavia. Explain the discussion on page 65 about the winter night skies.

Chapter 8   "There Has Been a Death"—Pages 67-73

Vocabulary
   haze 67   ruefully 69   specter 69   gesturing 69

Discussion Questions
1. Why is the joke about relocating butter gray humor? *(It is a funny comment and provokes a funny scene but is also a reminder of the German occupation.)*

2. What do Mama and the girls do during the day while Henrik is fishing? *(Play in the meadows and collect dried wild flowers, and clean and polish Henrik's house.)*

3. What is the odd reference Henrik makes to a "day for fishing"? *(Answers vary, but may suggest the unclearness of the comment and its strangeness when Henrik goes fishing every day.)* Make some predictions and guesses about what Henrik means.

4. What is so strange about Great-aunt Birte? *(Henrik announces that there will be a wake for her but Annemarie has never heard of her and thinks she doesn't exist.)*

5. What is the mood at the end of Chapter 8? *(mysterious)*

Supplementary Activities
1. From whose viewpoint is *Number the Stars* written? How do you know? Prepare a class definition of viewpoint.

2. Prepare an attribute web for Uncle Henrik.

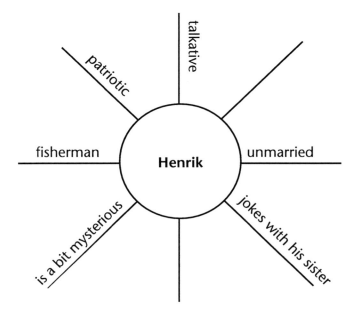

Chapter 9   "Why Are You Lying?"—Pages 74-81

Vocabulary
deftly 75	dismayed 76	cocked 76	hearse 77	wryly 77	trudged 78
wail 79	urgency 81				

Discussion Questions

1. What is Annemarie's confrontation with Uncle Henrik? *(She accuses him and Mama of lying to her about Great-aunt Birte.)*

2. How does Henrik answer Annemarie? *(He talks about bravery.)*

3. What is bravery? Think of a one-word synonym. Do you agree with Annemarie that it is easier to be brave if you do not know everything? Complete an attribute web on bravery. *(Save the web to use later in Chapter 16.)*

4. What is the reunion at the end of Chapter 9? *(Ellen's parents arrive at Uncle Henrik's as does Peter Neilsen.)* What is the mood of the reunion? *(restrained, apprehensive)* How does the author convey that mood? *(Directly by describing Peter's mood on page 81. Also indirectly by the lack of typical reunion festivities and joy.)*

Supplementary Activity

Authors convey moods in many ways—directly and indirectly. One indirect technique is to show a mood by contrast to another state of affairs, increasing the feeling by the comparison. For example, in Chapter 9, Lowry increases a mysterious, dangerous feeling by the implied comparison of a real wake to the events in the chapter. Look for other examples in this book and in other books. (Pages 74-75, Pastoral scene milking the cow and Annemarie learning about bravery; pages 69-71, Girls playing happily in fields and preparations for "a day for fishing.")

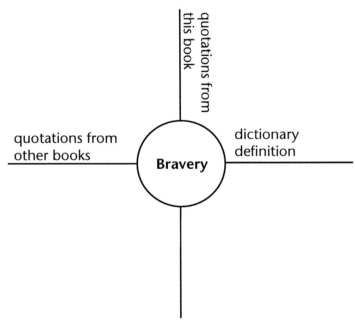

Chapter 10   "Let Us Open the Casket"—Pages 82-87

Vocabulary
surge 82   staccato 83   condescending 84   strode 86

Discussion Questions
1. What awakened Annemarie from dozing in the corner of the living room? *(The sounds of the soldiers who came to investigate the people gathering at the house.)*

2. How is Annemarie called upon to be brave? *(The soldier asks her who died and she must lie in her answer.)* How do you think she felt at that moment? *(Answers vary.)*

3. How does Mama divert the soldiers from opening the casket? *(by talking of possible contamination from a corpse which died of typhus)* What is typhus? *(An acute infectious disease caused by several species of Rickettsia, transmitted by lice and fleas.)*

4. How does Peter help the others relax and calm down after the soldiers left? *(He reads a Psalm to the group.)*

5. Why do you think the Psalm is important? *(Lowry took her title from the words of the Psalm. Annemarie thinks about the immense size of the sky and of the world and the individual stars and people in it. The size and cruelness of the world are significant as she tries to make sense of her place in the difficult times in which she lives.)*

Supplementary Activities
1. Investigate Psalm 147 from which the passage in the book comes. Discuss with parents what it means.

2. Dramatize this chapter.

Chapter 11 "Will We See You Again Soon, Peter?"—Pages 88-94

Vocabulary
protruding 91   commotion 93   misshapen 93

Discussion Questions
1. What was in the coffin? *(Blankets and clothing which Peter distributed to the "silent people in the room.")*

2. What does Peter give to the baby? *(Some liquid to make her sleep and not cry.)*

3. What does Peter give Mr. Rosen? *(an important packet for Henrik)*

4. How has Peter's station in the family changed? Cite examples from the book to support your answer. *(Peter calls Mrs. Johansen by her first name as he gives directions. Peter seems to be "in charge." When the situation becomes tense for the Rosens, Mama and Papa say they'll ask Peter. The "silent people" defer to Peter's direction.)*

5. What does Annemarie discover about pride in Chapter 11? *(Pride isn't just objects or clothing but is a state of mind. The Rosens, though clothed in ill-fitting garments and frightened, are still proud. They stand straight and tall.)*

Supplementary Activities
1. Prepare a story map to review the story. (See page 7.)

2. Share what makes you proud in a short paragraph.

Chapter 12   "Where Was Mama?"—Pages 95-100

Discussion Questions
1. Why do you think Henrik chose this particular night to take the Rosens to Sweden? *(no moon so it would be darker)*

2. What was Ellen's promise to Annemarie when she left? *(to return someday)* Do you think Ellen kept her promise? *(Answers vary.)*

3. How does Annemarie spend the night? *(She dozes in a rocking chair downstairs waiting for her mother to return, worrying.)*

4. When and where does Annemarie find her mother? *(just before daylight, lying on the path)*

Supplementary Activity
Reread the first paragraph on page 98. Do you agree or not? Explain in a short discussion with a classmate. Then write your answer in a paragraph.

Chapter 13   "Run! As Fast As You Can!"—Pages 101-105

Vocabulary
faltered 101   winced 101   sprawling 102

Discussion Questions
1. How does Mama get into the house? *(by leaning on Annemarie and stopping to rest many times)*

2. What does Annemarie find in the grass at the foot of the steps? *(The packet Peter gave Mr. Rosen to give to Uncle Henrik.)*

3. How do you know the packet was important? *(Peter says so and Mama is very concerned that it wasn't taken to Henrik.)*

4. Why didn't Mama answer Annemarie's question about the packet? *(She judges it better for Annemarie not to know in case she would be questioned.)*

Chapter 14   "On the Dark Path"—Pages 106-112

Vocabulary

donned 106	peered 106	latticed 106	populated 108	vivid 108
wriggle 109	segment 110	brusque 110	prolong 111	tantalize 111
taut 112				

Discussion Questions

1. How did Annemarie feel as she started on her way to deliver the packet to her uncle? *(apprehensive because of the danger from the soldiers; cold because of the weather and only her light sweater; tired because she didn't sleep well waiting for her mother; concerned because of her mother's injury)*

2. How did Annemarie comfort herself and occupy her mind as she walked to the boat? *(by thinking of a story she often told Kirsti as they cuddled in bed at night)* How do you occupy your mind on a walk? *(Answers vary.)* How do you keep your mind off danger? *(Answers vary.)*

3. Who is the real wolf for Annemarie as she approaches the harbor? *(four armed soldiers with two large dogs)*

Supplementary Activities

1. Following the narrative in the book, draw the path and scenery Annemarie passes as she goes on her errand.

2. What sounds would Annemarie have heard on her journey? Find direct references to sounds in the book and add your own ideas of possible sounds from your imagination. Generate a class list of the sounds and then reread the chapter with sound effects.

Chapter 15   "My Dogs Smell Meat!"—Pages 113-119

Vocabulary
enrage 114	consumed 115	withering 116	insolently 116
caustic 118	subsided 118	strident 118	

Discussion Questions

1. How does Annemarie act in talking with the soldiers? *(like a "silly little girl")*

2. Why do you think Annemarie would be particularly thankful to have Kirsti as a sister? *(When confronted by the soldiers, she just thought how Kirsti would act in each situation and then behaved that way.)*

3. What is the manner of the soldiers toward Annemarie? *(unpleasant, domineering, bossy, ridiculing her and the lunch)*

4. Why didn't the soldiers take the packet from Annemarie? *(They didn't recognize the packet of a handkerchief as anything important.)*

5. How did Annemarie fool the soldiers? *(She and her mother had concocted a reasonable cover story. Annemarie fooled them into believing she was no threat or problem because she was silly.)*

Supplementary Activity
The difference between appearance and reality is important in this chapter. Generate a listing of things and events that have a different appearance and reality from the story and from your own experiences. For example, the coffin in the story *appears* to be a burial box, but in *reality*, it's a container for coats and other things. Also, Great-aunt Birte's funeral *appears* to be a family funeral, but is in *reality* an opportunity for those leaving for Sweden to assemble. Choose one pairing to explain in a short paragraph or with a picture.

Chapter 16   "I Will Tell You Just a Little"—Pages 120-127

Vocabulary
warily 120   confronting 124

Discussion Questions
1. How has the mood of the book changed at the start of Chapter 16? *(The characters are laughing about Annemarie milking or trying to milk Blossom.)*

2. How does Annemarie's milking lesson proceed? *(Uncle Henrik doesn't really instruct her on milking technique. As he milked Blossom himself, he talked to Annemarie a little about the Rosens' escape.)*

3. What additional insights on bravery does Lowry give in this chapter? *(On page 123, "That's all that <u>brave</u> means—not thinking about the dangers. Just thinking about what you must do." Peter is a brave Resistance fighter.)*

4. What was the importance of the handkerchief Annemarie took to her uncle? *(The handkerchief had a chemical on it to destroy the dogs' sense of smell. When the soldiers checked Uncle Henrik's boat with the dogs, the dogs didn't find the Jews hidden beneath the floor boards.)*

Supplementary Activity
Research: Why does Uncle Henrik say Sweden will not be taken by the Nazis? Is it truth?

Chapter 17   "All This Long Time"—Pages 128-132

Vocabulary
devastating 129   bleak 129

Discussion Questions
1. Fill in the next two years in Copenhagen until the war ends. *(Danish people tended plants and looked after the empty Jewish apartments. The Resistance efforts continued and Peter Neilsen was executed by the Germans.)*

2. What was the truth of Lise's death? *(She was run down by German occupying troops when she fled from a Resistance meeting.)*

3. How does Lowry conclude the novel with the return of a symbol? *(Annemarie looks into the trunk with Lise's trousseau and finds Ellen's Star of David. She asks her father to repair the necklace and decides to wear it herself until Ellen returns.)*

Supplementary Activity
There are several different plot lines used in different books. This book has a plot with rising action and then a short amount of resolution (called denouement) after the climax. Here is the graph.

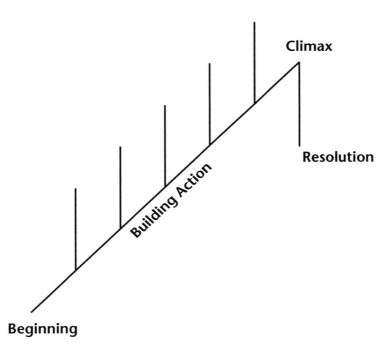

Using the plot line provided on the next page, fill in significant parts of this book. Use chapters and events to designate particular parts of the book.

Graphing Plot Lines

Climax:

Resolution:

Building Action

Beginning:

Afterword Pages 133-137

Vocabulary

deprivation 133	integrity 133	compassion 135	permeated 136
orchestrated 136	sabotage 136		

Discussion Questions

1. Fill in this chart indicating which items were fiction (made up by the author) and which were non-fiction (really happened):

	Fiction	Non-Fiction
Annemarie Johansen		
Christian X		
Sinking the Danish Navy		
Escape by Danish Jews to Sweden		
Handkerchief to disable dogs' sense of smell		
Peter Neilsen		
Tivoli Gardens		

2. Why would an author include an Afterword? *(to give background detail)* Why is it particularly appropriate for this book? *(The historical setting of the book is critical to the plot. Readers wonder about authenticity and which items were from the writer's imagination.)*

Concluding Activities

1. At the end, Lowry speaks of "the gift of a world of human decency." What does the quoted phrase mean and what does it explain about the purpose of the book.

2. In a short paragraph or talk, explain why the book is either 1) historical fiction, or 2) an adventure story, or 3) a girls' book, or 4) a mystery story, or 5) focused on bravery, or 6) focused on friendship.

3. Pretending you are Ellen Rosen, write an essay about what my best friend did for me.

4. Interview someone who lived during World War II to find out about the war and how it affected your interviewee. *(Probably anyone born before 1936 will have some memories of World War II.)*

5. Choose one of the books on the bibliography list to read. Compare it to *Number the Stars* using a Venn diagram to record your observations.

Vocabulary Activities

1. Speed Dictionary: Post vocabulary challenge words. Students look up definitions in dictionaries, striving for speed. Team play is a possible adaptation.

2. Students define words, then play twenty questions giving characteristics for classmates to guess the word. For example, vegetable soup *(served for lunch, with crackers, hot, served in a bowl, mostly liquid, food)*.

3. Record new words on 3 x 5 cards to study at odd moments. Record definitions on one side and sentence where word occurred on the other. Use as flashcards.

4. Each student chooses (or is given) a word to compose an advertisement to "sell" his word.

5. Students sort the vocabulary words according to part of speech *(describers, names, actions)*.

6. Be a detective. The teacher writes a definition on board. Students match with their individual vocabulary words.

7. Write the words the way they feel.   little   **Big**

8. Draw a face to describe the emotion of your vocabulary word.

9. Students generate on-going word banks on long strips of paper or in notebooks. Possible categories include sensory words *(hearing, touching, smelling, seeing)*, names, actions, funny words, and survival words.

Bibliography of Books on Similar Themes

The Cage by Ruth Minsky Sender
Chernowitz! by Frank Arrick
The Devil in Vienna by Doris Argel
Diary of Anne Frank by Anne Frank
The Dolphin Crossing by Jill Paton Walsh
The Endless Steppe by Esther Hautzig
The Fifth Son by Elie Wiesel
A Hidden Childhood by Frida Scheps Weinstein
I Am Fifteen—And I Don't Want to Die by Christine Arnathy
I Am Rosemarie by Marietta D. Moskin
Journey to America by Sonia Levitin
My Hundred Children by Lena Kuchler-Silberman
North to Freedom by Anne Holm
The Story of Harriet Tubman, Conductor of the Underground Railroad by Kate McMullan
Upon the Head of the Goat by Aranka Siegal
The Upstairs Room by Johanna Reiss
When Hitler Stole Pink Rabbit by Judith Kerr

Assessment for *Number the Stars*

Assessment is an on-going process, more than a quiz at the end of the book. Points may be added to show the level of achievement. When an item is completed, the teacher and the student check it.

Name _____ Date _____

Student   **Teacher**

_____   _____   1. Write a journal that Annemarie or Ellen might have kept.

_____   _____   2. Make an attribute web for one of the characters. Compare your web with a classmate's web. (See pages 12-14 of this guide.)

_____   _____   3. Participate in a drama activity.

_____   _____   4. Identify the geographic locations mentioned in the novel. Draw a map marking the approximate distances between locations.

_____   _____   5. Make a list of symbols. Choose one to explain in a short paragraph.

_____   _____   6. Prepare a story map to review the story. (See page 7 of this guide.)

_____   _____   7. Research treatment of the Jewish people in World War II.

_____   _____   8. Make a list of sounds in the book.

_____   _____   9. Make a collage about bravery. You may use magazine cut-outs, drawings, and real objects. Write a paragraph explaining your collage.

_____   _____   10. Write a self-assessment about your work, behavior, and effort on this unit.

Note: Additional study questions, and quizzes and tests are available in the Novel Units Student Packet for *Number the Stars*.